SEA CREATURES
Knitting & Crochet Patterns

Designed & Written by
Angela M. Foster

SEA CREATURES
Knitting & Crochet Patterns
Patterns designed and written by
Angela M. Foster

ISBN-13: 978-1463511999
ISBN-10: 146351199X

Copyright © 2011 by Angela M. Foster

Published by Angela M. Foster

All rights reserved.

No part of this book may be reproduced or distributed

in any form or by any means, or stored in a database retrieval system,

without prior written permission from Angela M. Foster.

Dedicated to my wonderful son, Joseph, who has an undying love for the ocean and it's inhabitants.

CONTENTS

How to read the graph/chart..11

Basic materials needed for projects..13

Wash / Face / Dish Cloth Pattern
    Knitting..15
    Crochet...15

Bath Mat Pattern
    Knitting...15,16
    Crochet...16

Place Mat Pattern
    Knitting...16,17
    Crochet...17

Throw Pillow Pattern
    Knitting...17,18
    Crochet...18

Blanket Patterns
    Infant..18
    Toddler...19
    Twin...19
    Full...19
    Queen / King..20

Graphs / Charts
    Barnacle...21
    Clam...22
    Crab...23
    Dolphin..24
    Electric Eel...25
    Horseshoe Crab..26
    Jellyfish..27
    Lobster...28

Manatee..29
Manta Ray...30
Octopus..31
Orca Whale...32
Plankton...33
Salt Water Crocodile..34
Sand Dollar...35
Sea Anemone..36
Sea Cucumber...37
Sea Horse..38
Sea Snail..39
Sea Snake..40
Sea Turtle..41
Sea Urchin...42
Sea Worm..43
Shark (Great White)...44
Shrimp...45
Squid..46
Starfish..47
Sting Ray...48
Notes..49,50

READING GRAPHS/CHARTS

How to read the graphs/charts in this book:

Read the knitting/crochet chart right to left on row 1. (The first dot in the lower right corner equates to the first stitch on your left hand needle or your 1st stitch on the chain.) Progress across the row, changing colors when needed.

Row 2 will be read left to right, progress as row 1.

Repeat rows 1 and 2 for the whole chart.

You should keep in mind that knitting/crochet charts are a visual representation of the right side of the knitting/crocheting. As such in knitting, you will need to knit every odd row (right side) and purl every even row (wrong side) <u>unless otherwise stated</u>. In crochet, you will need to keep in mind every odd row is the right side of the piece and every even row is the wrong side of the piece.

Charted knitting/crochet is often easier to keep track of than standard notation and the visual image of a knitting/crochet chart is more appealing to many knitters/crocheters.

HINT: The biggest thing to remember while doing graphs/charts is to pay close attention to which way you are going on it. You can easily do this by marking your rows as you go by placing check marks or symbols beside each row. Example: When on the first row, place a check mark (or any symbol) on the right hand side of that row. When you move to the second row, place a check mark (or any symbol) on the left hand side of that row. Keep repeating until whole chart is done.

BASIC MATERIALS

Knitting: 1 skein of worsted weight (#4 medium) yarn for each color needed.
Acrylic (i.e. Red Heart) can be used for all the patterns but dishcloths. 100% cotton (#4 medium) yarn should be used for dishcloths (try to match the yarn colors as much as possible or improvise).
Size 4 & 7 knitting needles.
Yarn needle.
Yarn bobbins (optional).

Crochet: 1 skein (for each color needed) of fingering/baby weight (#3 light) yarn for the washcloth and placemat patterns. And worsted weight (#4 medium) for the bath mat and throw pillow patterns.
Acrylic (i.e. Bernat Baby) can be used for all the patterns but dishcloths. 100% cotton (#3 light) yarn should be used for dishcloths (try to match the yarn colors as much as possible or improvise)
Size D & G crochet hooks.
Yarn needle.
Yarn bobbins (optional).

WASH / FACE / DISH CLOTH
Knitted Version

SIZE: approximately 12" by 12" square

GAUGE: 5 st st = 1" , 7 rows = 1"

TO BEGIN: Use size 4 needles to loosely cast on 60 sts with light blue #4 yarn.
Rows 1-7: knit
Row 8: knit 5, knit 1st row of graph/chart, knit 5 (right side)
Row 9: knit 5, purl 2nd row of graph/chart, knit 5 (wrong side)
Rows 10-77: repeat rows 8 & 9
Rows 78-84: knit

FINISHING: Loosely cast off. Cut yarn. Weave in all ends.

Crochet Version

SIZE: approximately 12" by 12" square

GAUGE: 4.5 sc = 1" , 6 sc rows = 1"

TO BEGIN: Use size D hook. Chain 55 with light blue #3 yarn.
Row 1: single crochet across (54 sc)
Row 2: sc 2, sc 1st row of graph/chart, sc 2 (right side)
Row 3: sc 2, sc 2nd row of graph/chart, sc 2 (wrong side)
Rows 4-71: repeat rows 2 & 3
Row 72: sc across

FINSIHING: Single crochet once around all the edges. Cut yarn. Weave in all ends.

BATH MAT
Knitted Version

SIZE: approximately 23" high by 32" wide

GAUGE: 4.5 st st = 1" , 6.5 rows = 1"

TO BEGIN: Use size 7 needles to loosely cast on 144 sts with light blue #4 yarn.
Rows 1-14: knit
Row 15: knit 10, knit 124, knit 10

Row 16: knit 10, purl 124, knit 10
Rows 17-39: repeat rows 15 & 16
Row 40: knit 10, purl 37, purl 1st row of graph/chart, purl 37, knit 10 (wrong side)
Row 41: knit 10, knit 37, knit 2nd row of graph/chart, knit 37, knit 10 (right side)
Rows 42-109: repeat rows 40 & 41
Row: 110: knit 10, purl 124, knit 10
Row 111: knit 10, knit 124, knit 10
Rows 112-134: repeat rows 42 & 43
Rows 135-148: knit

FINISHING: Loosely cast off. Cut yarn. Weave in all ends.

Crochet Version

SIZE: approximately 23" high by 32" wide

GAUGE: 3.5 sc = 1" , 4 sc rows = 1"

TO BEGIN: Use size G hook. Chain 113 with light blue #4 yarn.
Rows 1-11: single crochet across (112 sc)
Row 12: sc 31, sc 1st row of graph/chart, sc 31 (right side)
Row 13: sc 31, sc 2nd row of graph/chart, sc 31 (wrong side)
Rows 14-81: repeat rows 12 & 13
Rows 82-92: sc across

FINSIHING: Single crochet once around all the edges. Cut yarn. Weave in all ends.

PLACE MAT
Knitted Version

SIZE: approximately 13" high by 19" wide

GAUGE: 4.5 st st = 1" , 6.5 rows = 1"

TO BEGIN: Use size 7 needles to loosely cast on 86 sts with light blue #4 yarn.
Rows 1-7: knit
Row 8: knit 5, knit 13, knit 1st row of graph/chart, knit 13, knit 5 (right side)
Row 9: knit 5, purl 13, purl 2nd row of graph/chart, purl 13, knit 5 (wrong side)
Rows 10-77: repeat rows 8 & 9
Rows 78-84: knit

FINISHING: Loosely cast off. Cut yarn. Weave in all ends.

Crochet Version

SIZE: approximately 13" high by 19" wide

GAUGE: 4.5 sc = 1" , 6 sc rows = 1"

TO BEGIN: Use size D hook. Chain 85 with light blue #3 yarn.
Rows 1-4: single crochet across (84 sc)
Row 5: sc 17, sc 1st row of graph/chart, sc 17 (right side)
Row 6: sc 17, sc 2nd row of graph/chart, sc 17 (wrong side)
Rows 7-74: repeat rows 5 & 6
Row 75-78: sc across

FINSIHING: Single crochet once around all the edges. Cut yarn. Weave in all ends.

THROW PILLOW
Knitted Version

SIZE: approximately 18" by 18" square

GAUGE: 4.5 st st = 1" , 6.5 rows = 1"

FRONT: Use size 7 needles to loosely cast on 82 sts with light blue #4 yarn.
Row 1: purl
Row 2: knit
Rows 3-24: repeat rows 1 & 2
Row 25: purl 16, purl 1st row of graph/chart, purl 16 (wrong side)
Row 26: knit 16, knit 2nd row of graph/chart, knit 16 (right side)
Rows 27-94: repeat rows 25 & 26
Row 95: purl
Row 96: knit
Rows 97-118: repeat rows 95 & 96
Loosely cast off. Cut yarn. Weave in all ends.

BACK: Use size 7 needles to loosely cast on 82 sts with light blue yarn.
Row 1: Purl (wrong side)
Row 2: knit (right side)
Rows 3-118: repeat rows 1 & 2
Loosely cast off. Cut yarn. Weave in all ends.

FINISHING: Place front and back together inside out. Sew together, leaving a 4" opening. Stuff. Sew up opening.

Crochet Version

SIZE: approximately 18" high by 18" wide

GAUGE: 3.5 sc = 1", 4 sc rows = 1"

FRONT: Use size G hook. Chain 65 with light blue #4 yarn.
Row 1: single crochet across (64 sc)
Row 2: sc 7, sc 1st row of graph/chart, sc 7 (right side)
Row 3: sc 7, sc 2nd row of graph/chart, sc 7 (wrong side)
Rows 4-71: repeat rows 2 & 3
Row 72: sc across
Cut yarn. Weave in all ends.

BACK: Use size G hook. Chain 65 with light blue #4 yarn.
Rows 1-72: single crochet across (64 sc)
Cut yarn. Weave in all ends.

FINISHING
Option 1: Place front and back together inside out. Sew together, leaving a 4" opening. Stuff. Sew up opening.

Option 2: Place front and back together outside right. Single crochet through both layers all the way around, leaving a 4" opening. Stuff. Close opening through both layers with single crochet. Place marker. Continue single (or half-double or double) crocheting in the round until edging/ruffle is as wide as u would like it.

BLANKETS
Knitting / Crochet Versions

INFANT (0-1 yrs): Size 2ft x 2ft. Make 4 of the wash/face/dish cloths. Place them as shown. Sew together.

TODDLER (1-5 yrs): Size 4ft x 4ft. Make 16 of the wash/face/dish cloths. Place them as shown. Sew together.

TWIN (5-13 yrs): Size 5ft x 6ft. Make 30 of the wash/face/dish cloths. Place them as shown. Sew together.

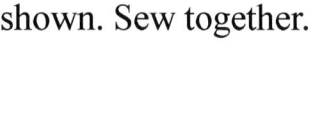

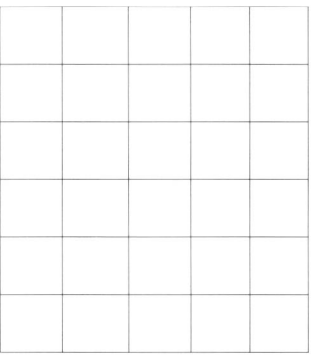

FULL (13 yrs-adult): Size 6ft x 6ft. Make 36 of the wash/face/dish cloths. Place them as shown. Sew together.

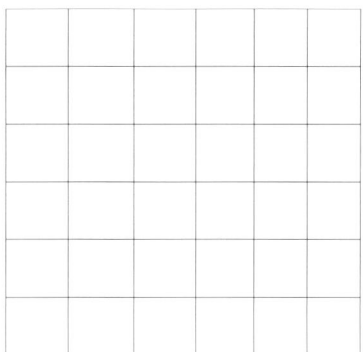

QUEEN/KING: Size 7ft x 7ft. Make 49 of the wash/face/dish cloths. Place them as shown. Sew together.

BARNACLE
GRAPH / CHART

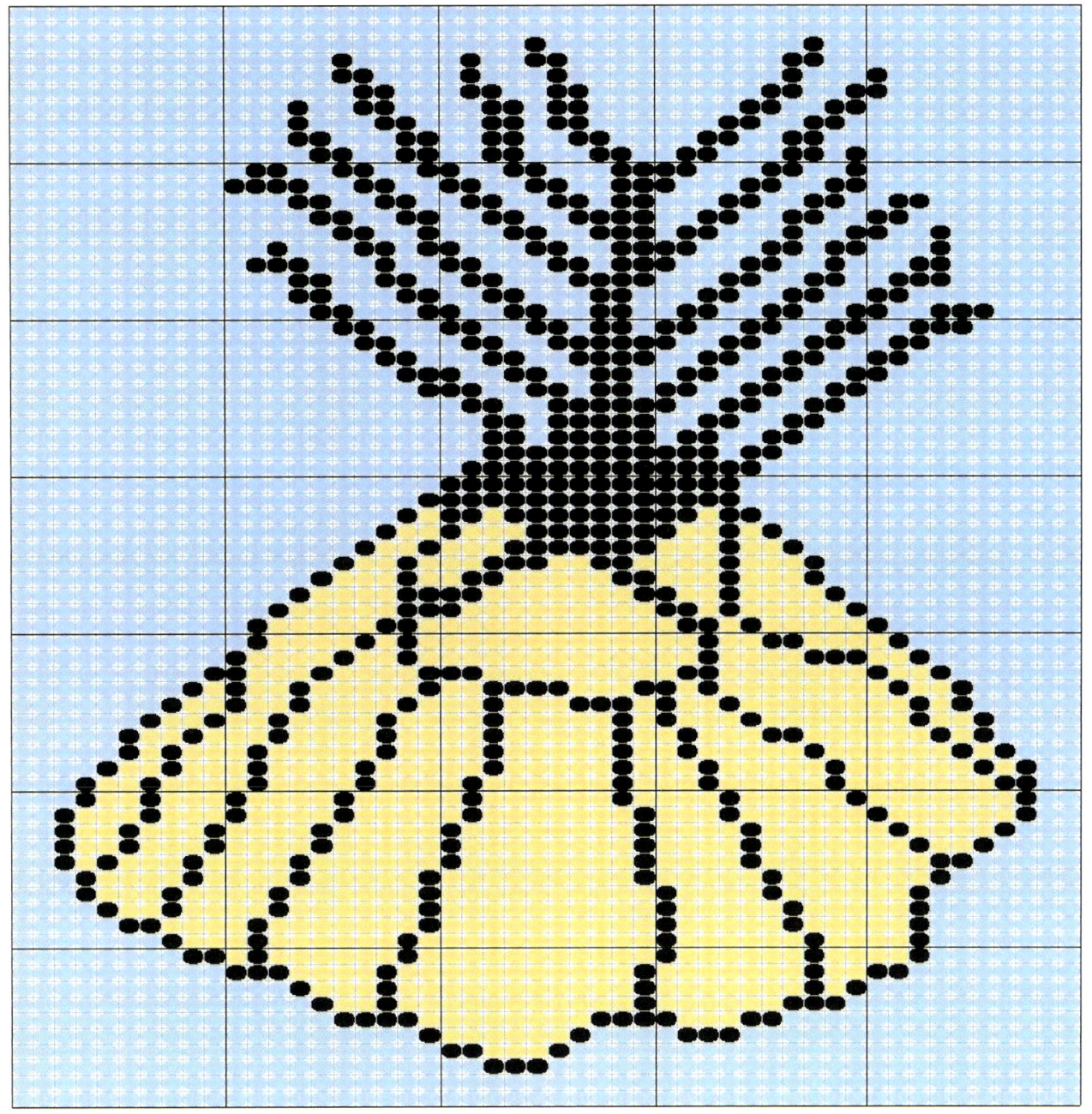

YARN COLORS

Light blue, black, and tan.

CLAM
GRAPH / CHART

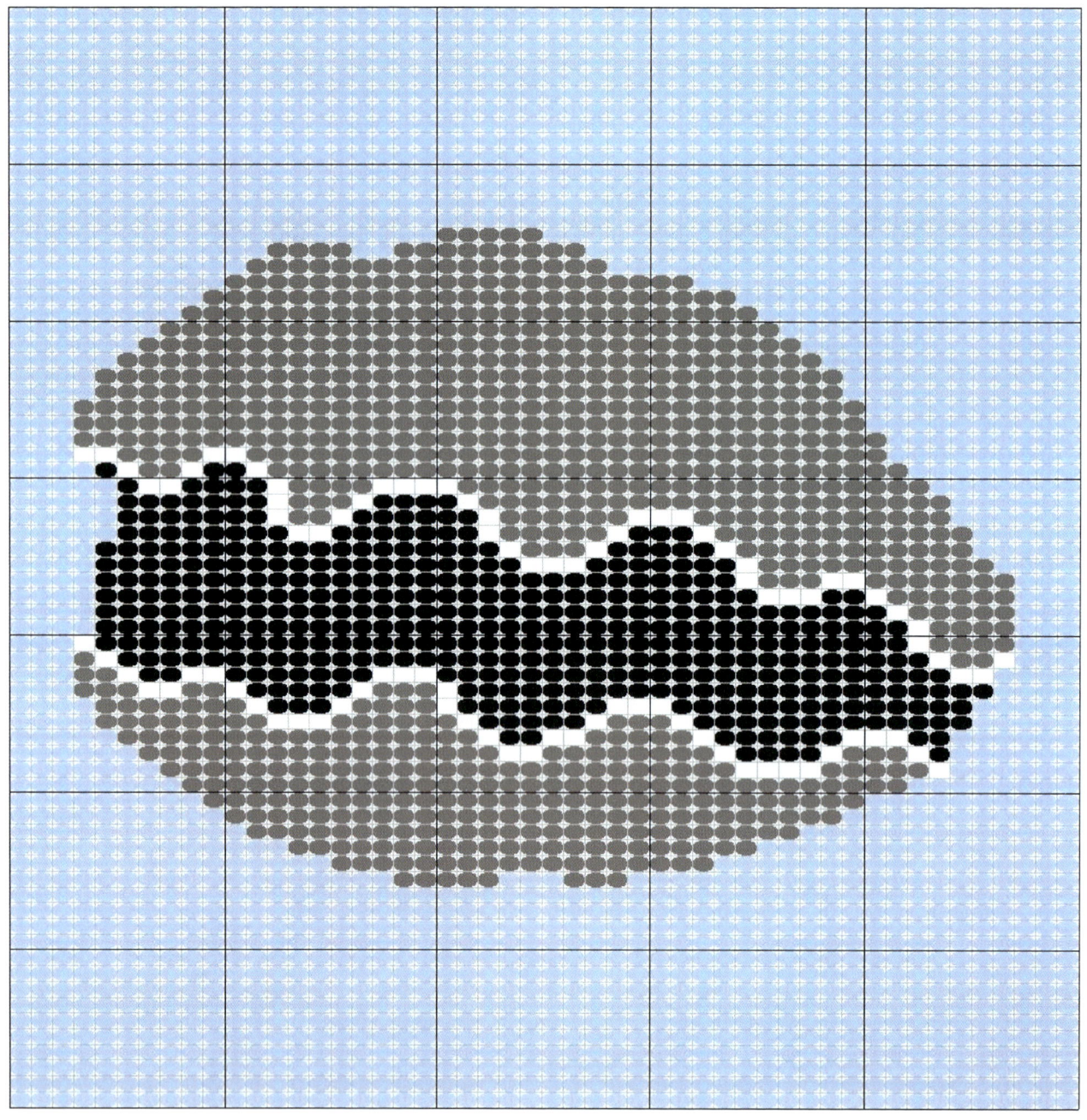

YARN COLORS

Light blue, black, gray and white.

CRAB
GRAPH / CHART

YARN COLORS

Light blue, black, and red.

DOLPHIN
GRAPH / CHART

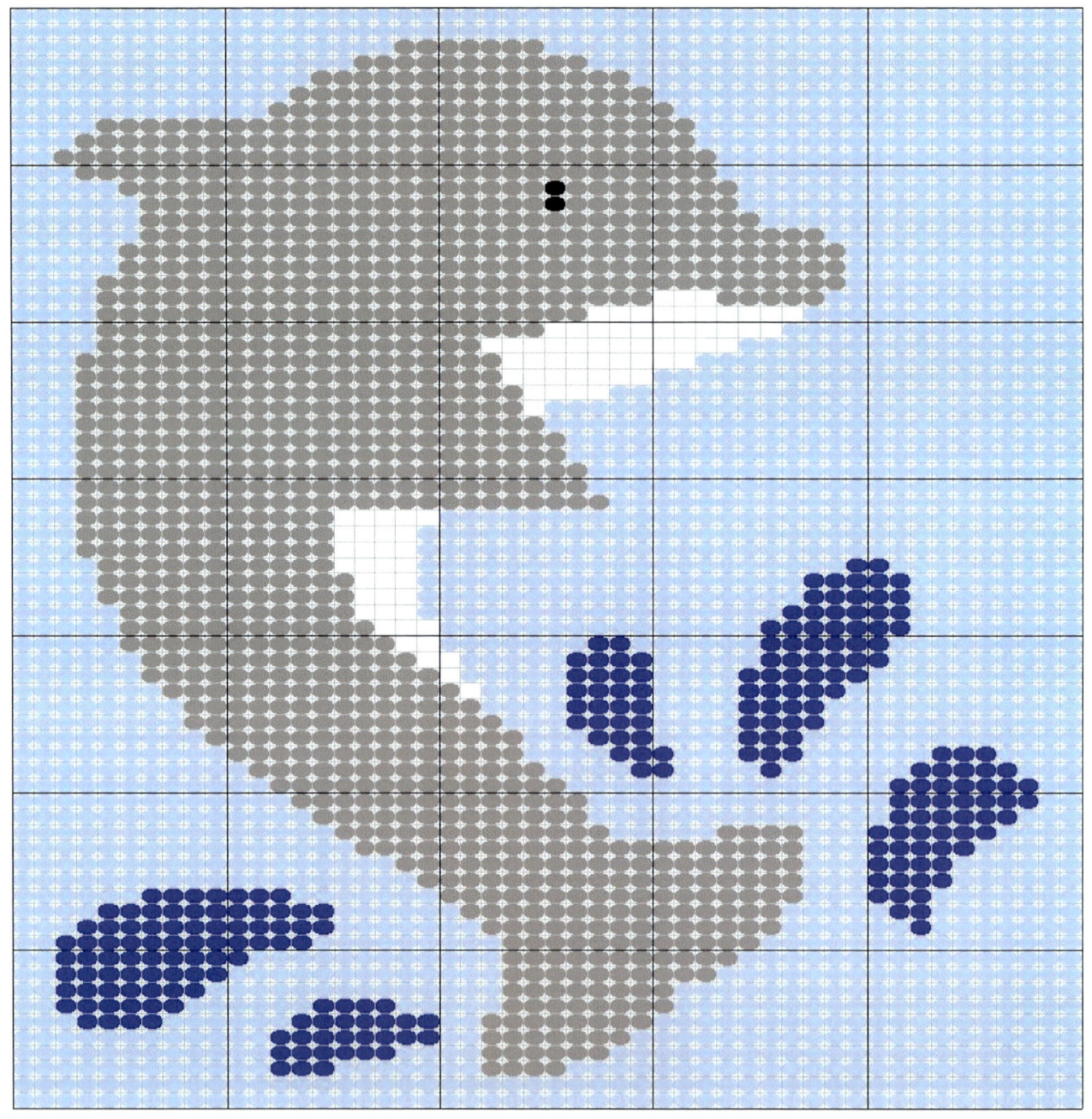

YARN COLORS

Light blue, blue, gray, white and black.

ELECTRIC EEL
GRAPH / CHART

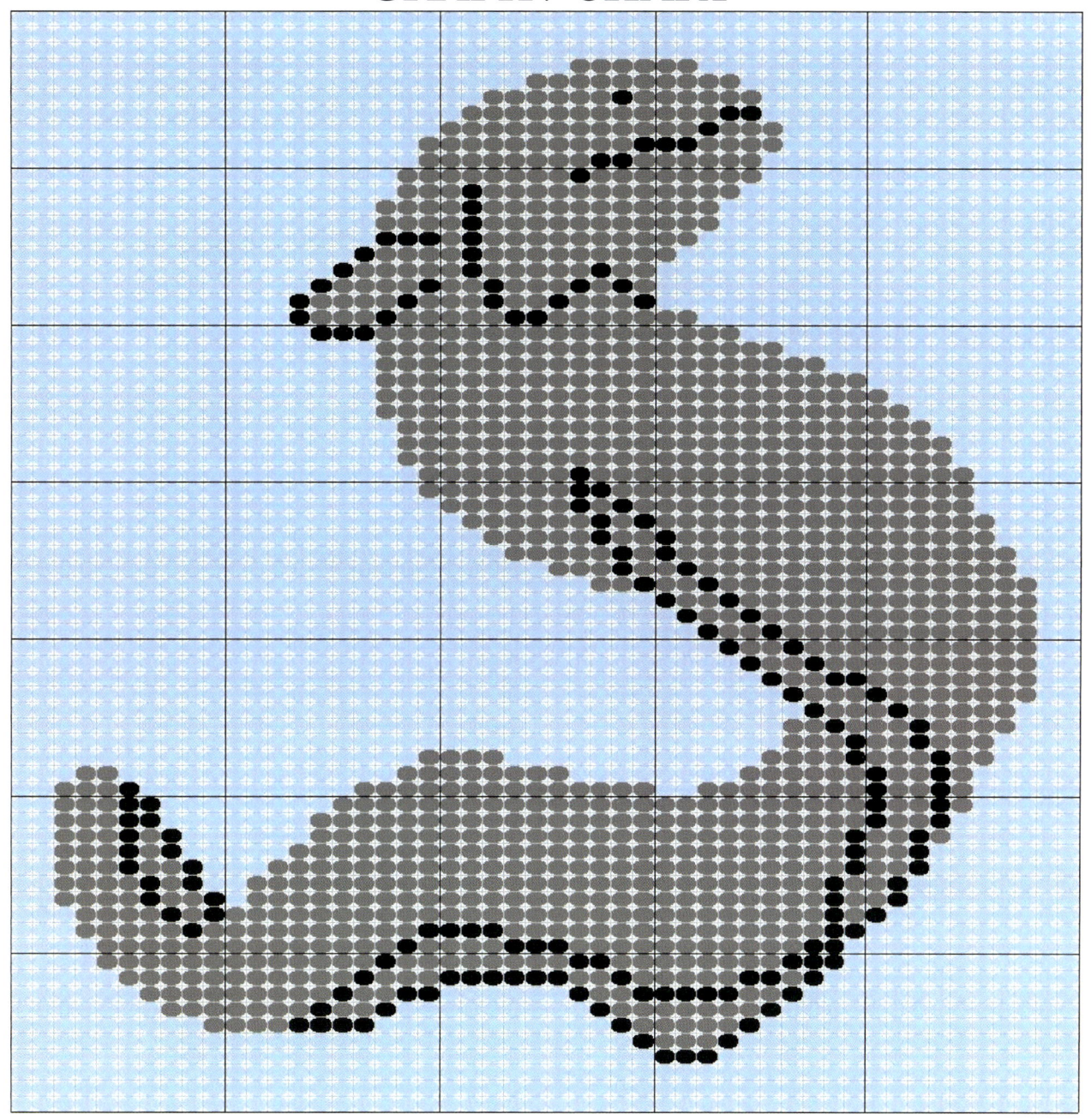

YARN COLORS

Light blue, black and gray.

HORSESHOE CRAB
GRAPH / CHART

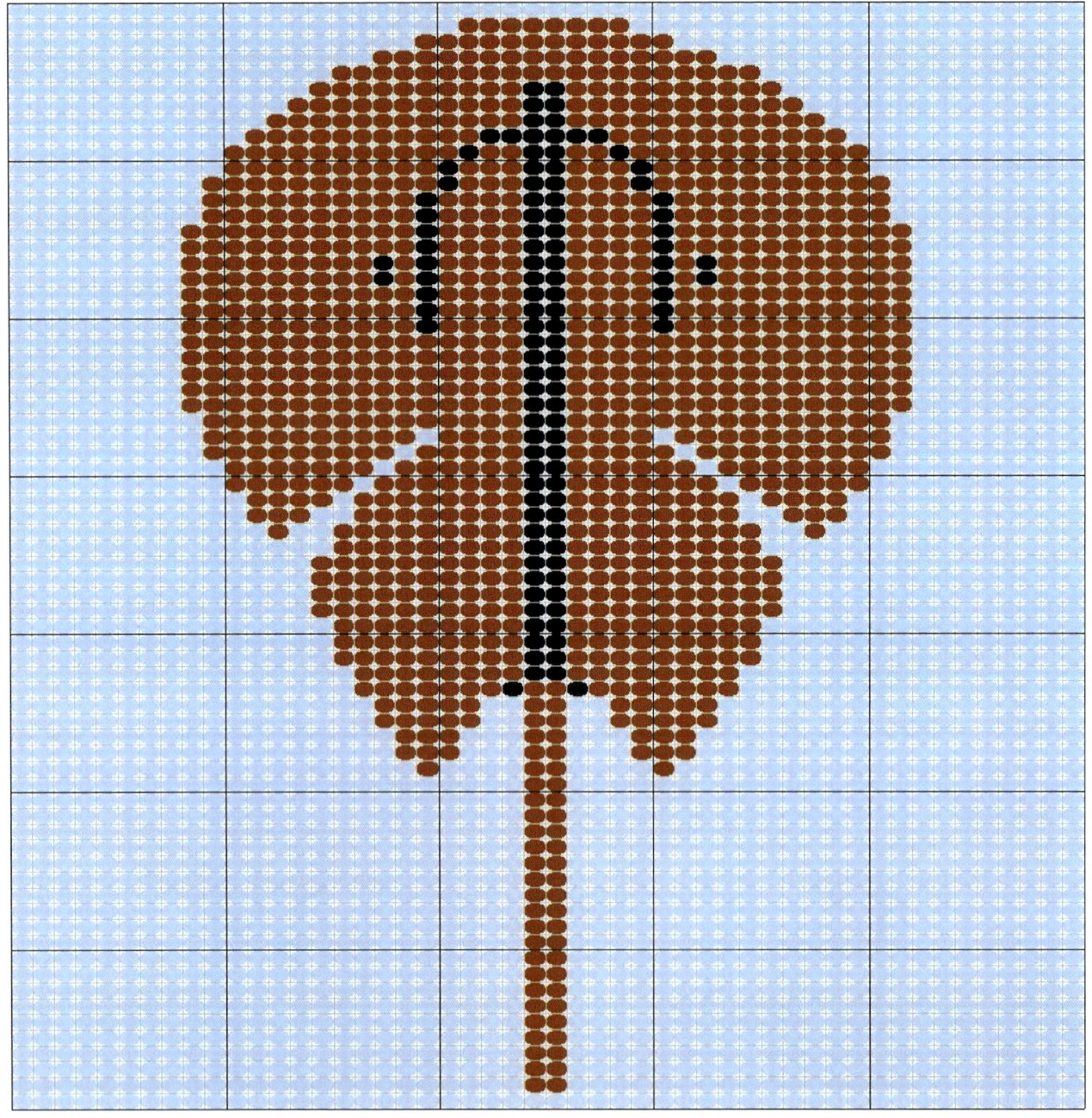

YARN COLORS

Light blue, black, and brown.

JELLYFISH
GRAPH / CHART

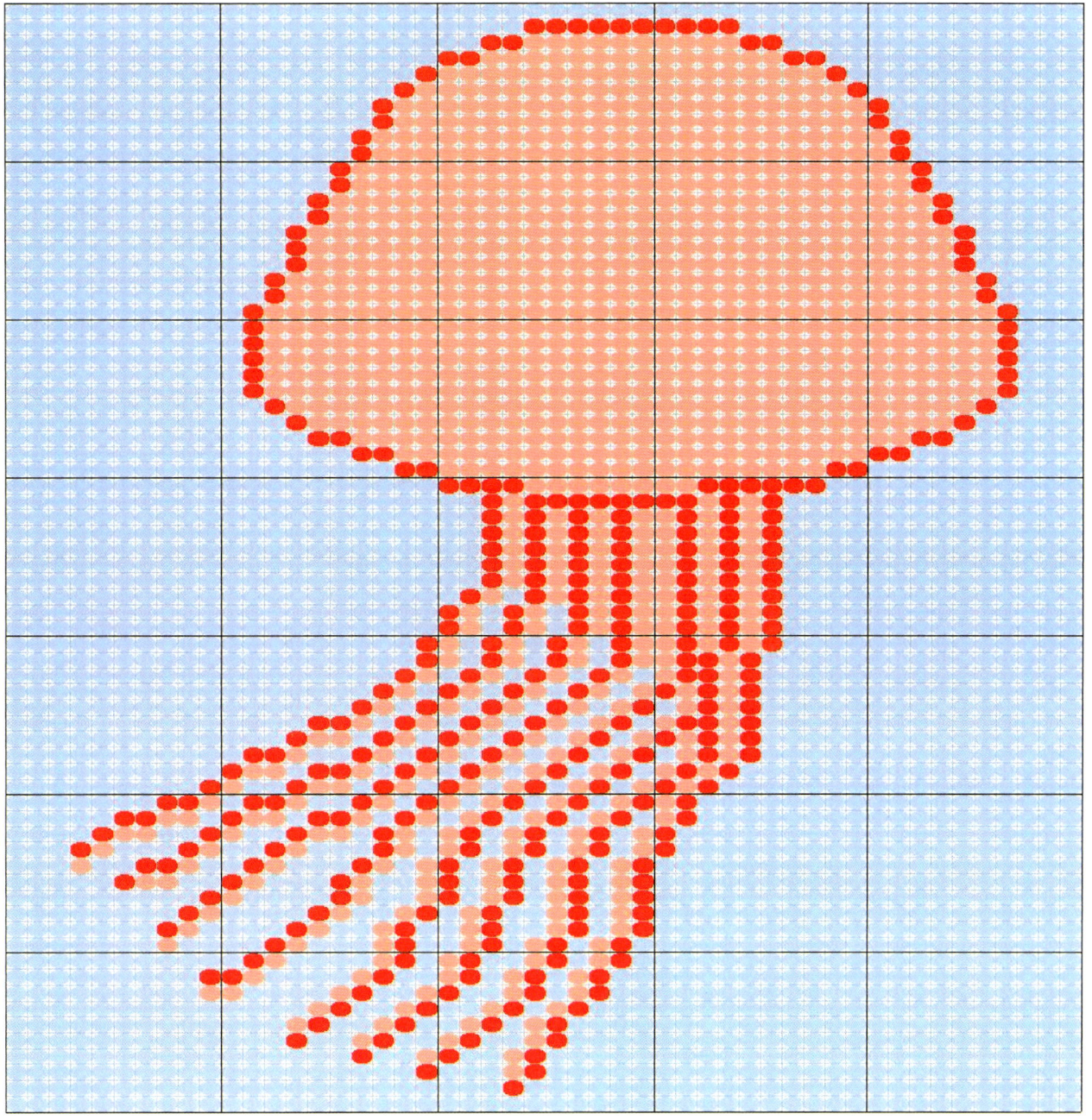

YARN COLORS

Light blue, pink and red.

LOBSTER
GRAPH / CHART

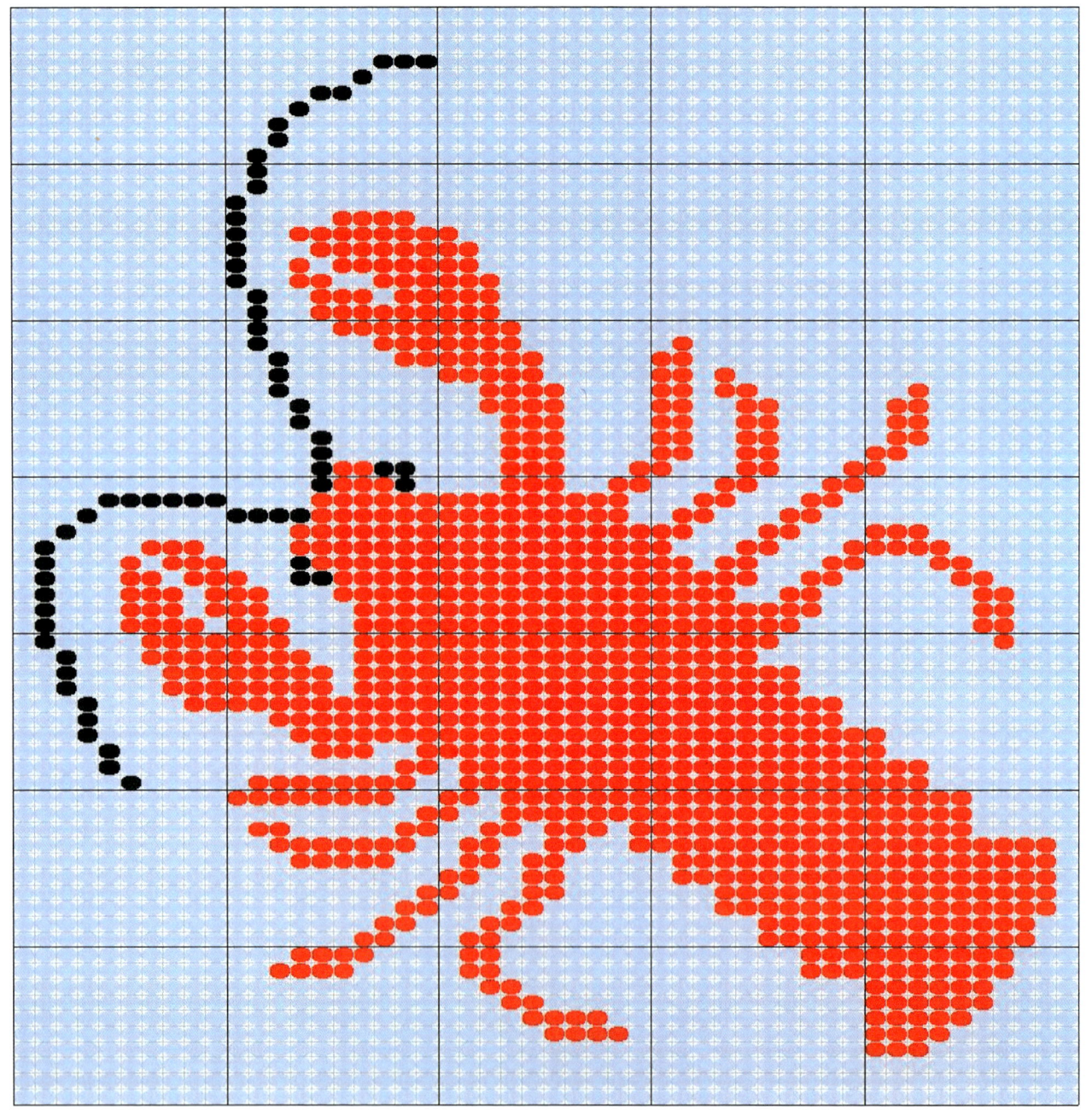

YARN COLORS

Light blue, black, and red.

MANATEE
GRAPH / CHART

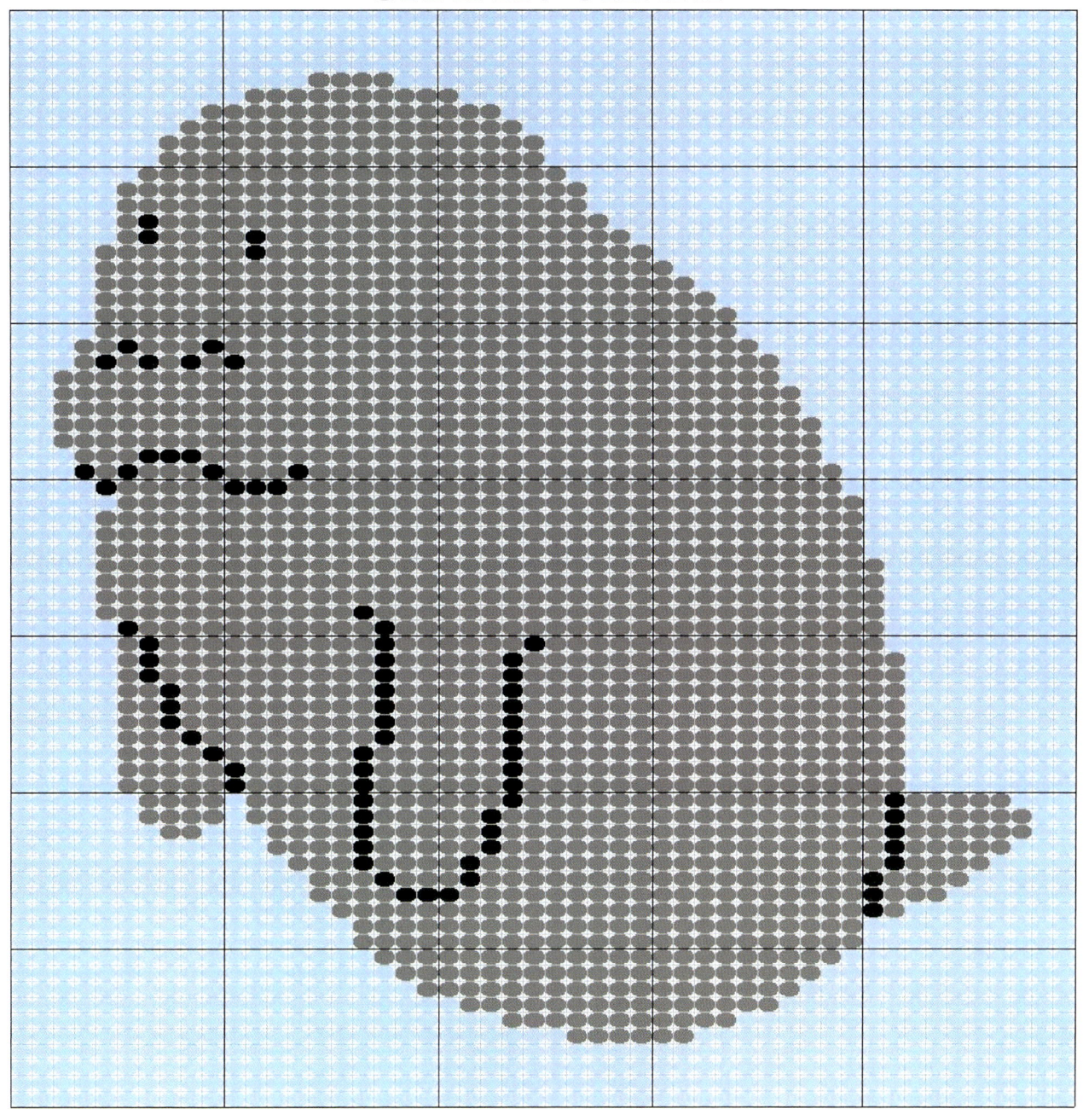

YARN COLORS

Light blue, black and gray.

MANTA RAY
GRAPH / CHART

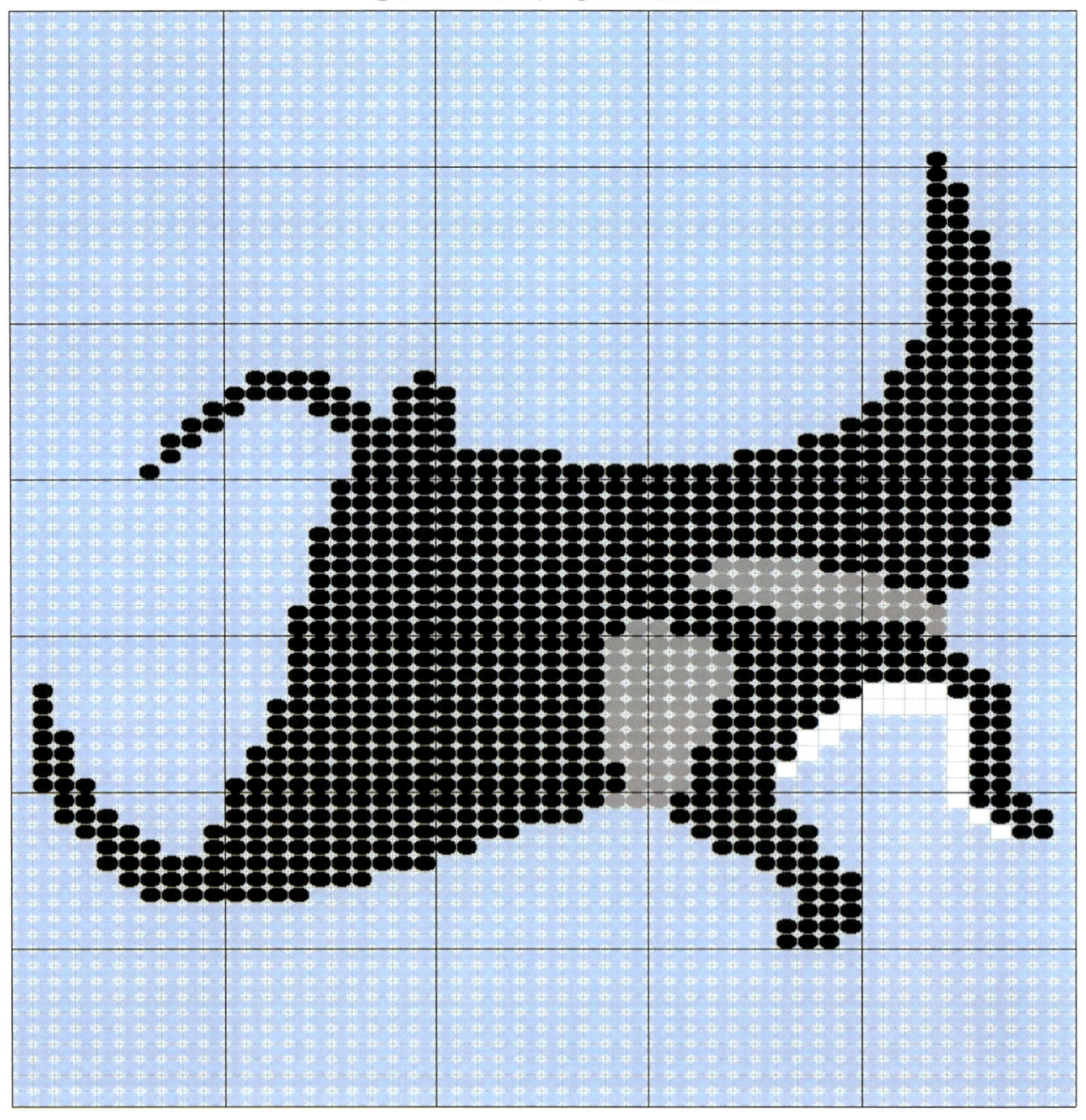

YARN COLORS

Light blue, black, white and gray.

OCTOPUS
GRAPH / CHART

YARN COLORS

Light blue, black, yellow and red.

ORCA WHALE
GRAPH / CHART

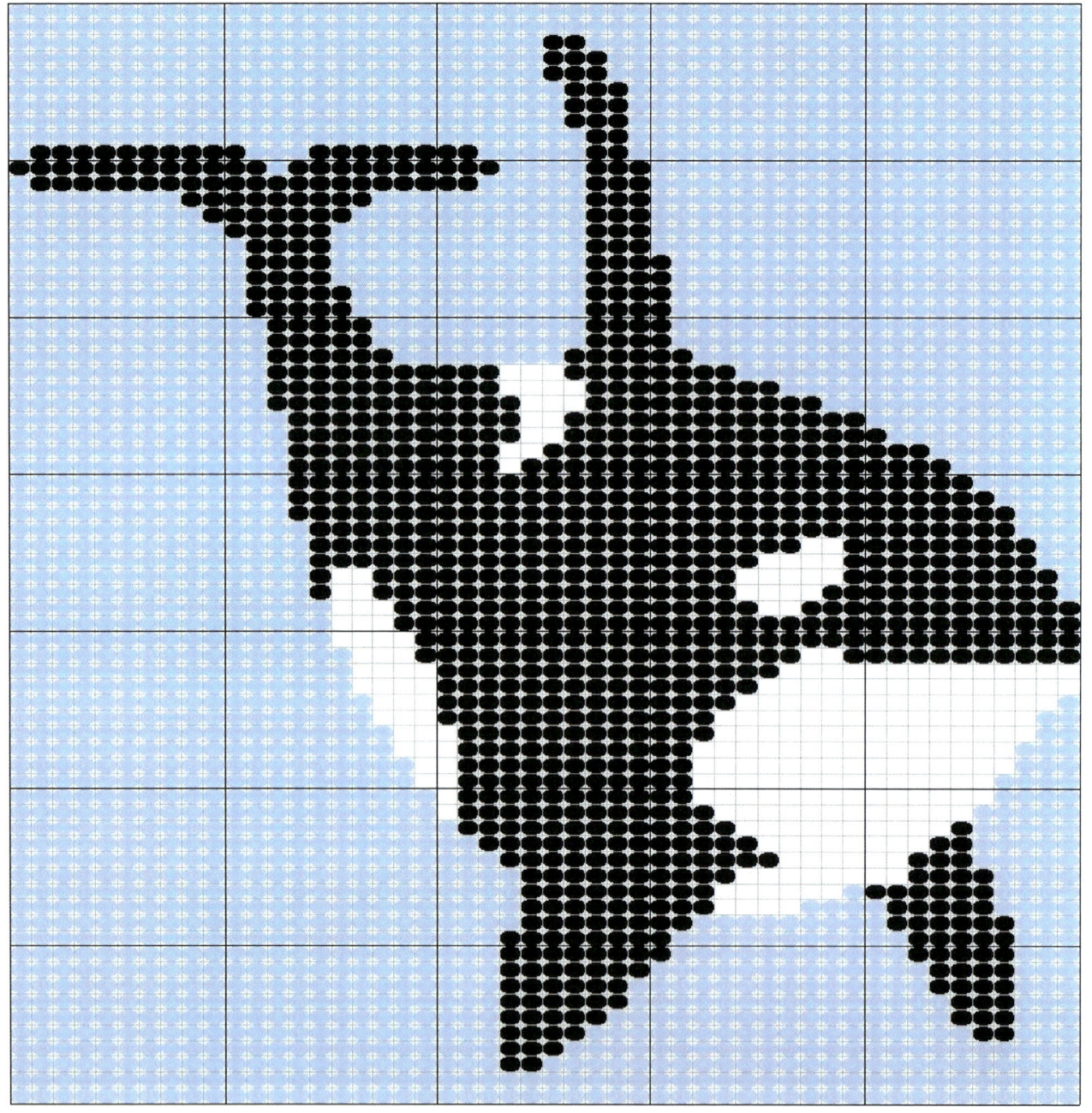

YARN COLORS

Light blue, black and white.

PLANKTON
GRAPH / CHART

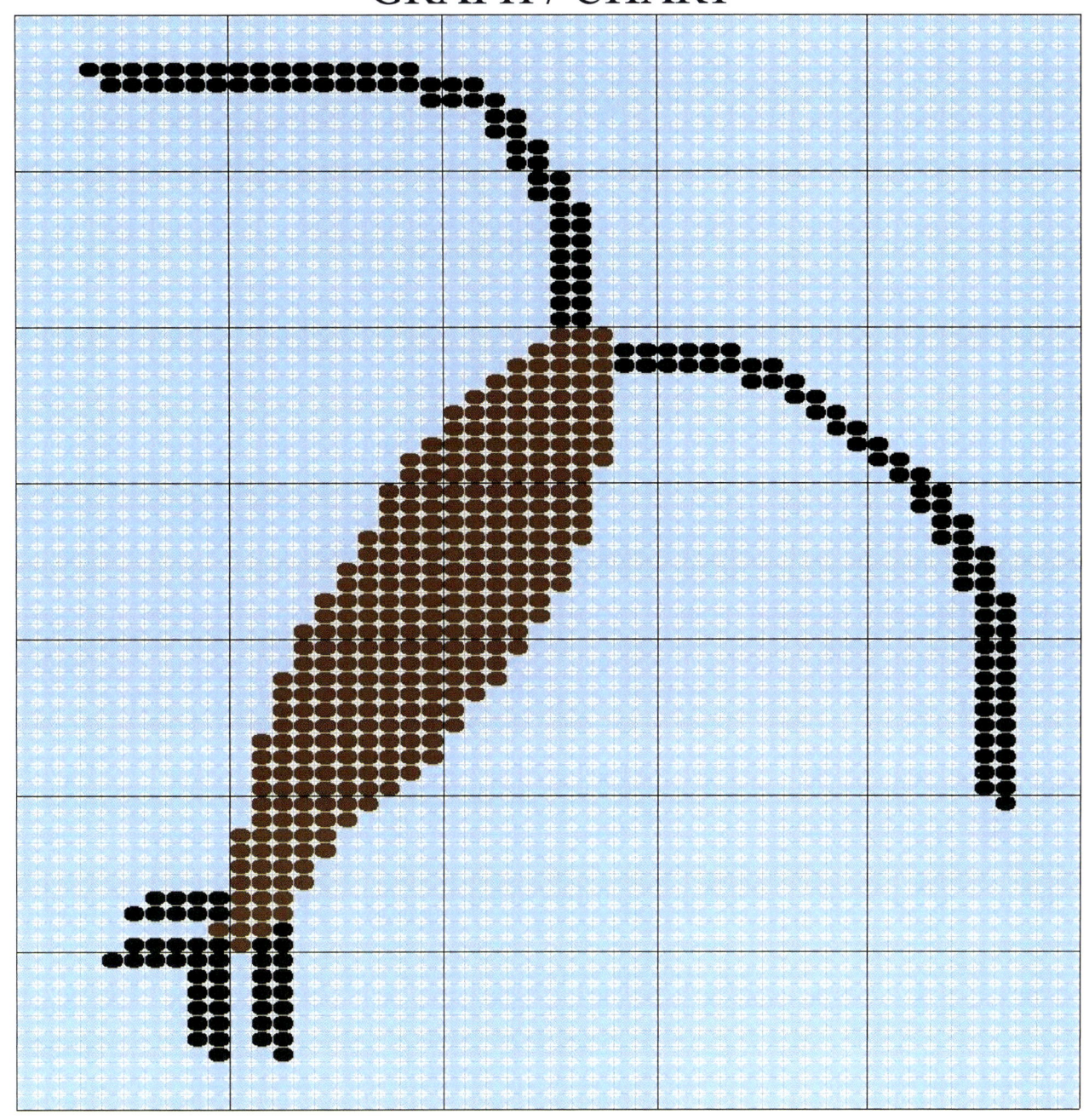

YARN COLORS

Light blue, black, and brown.

SALT WATER CROCODILE
GRAPH / CHART

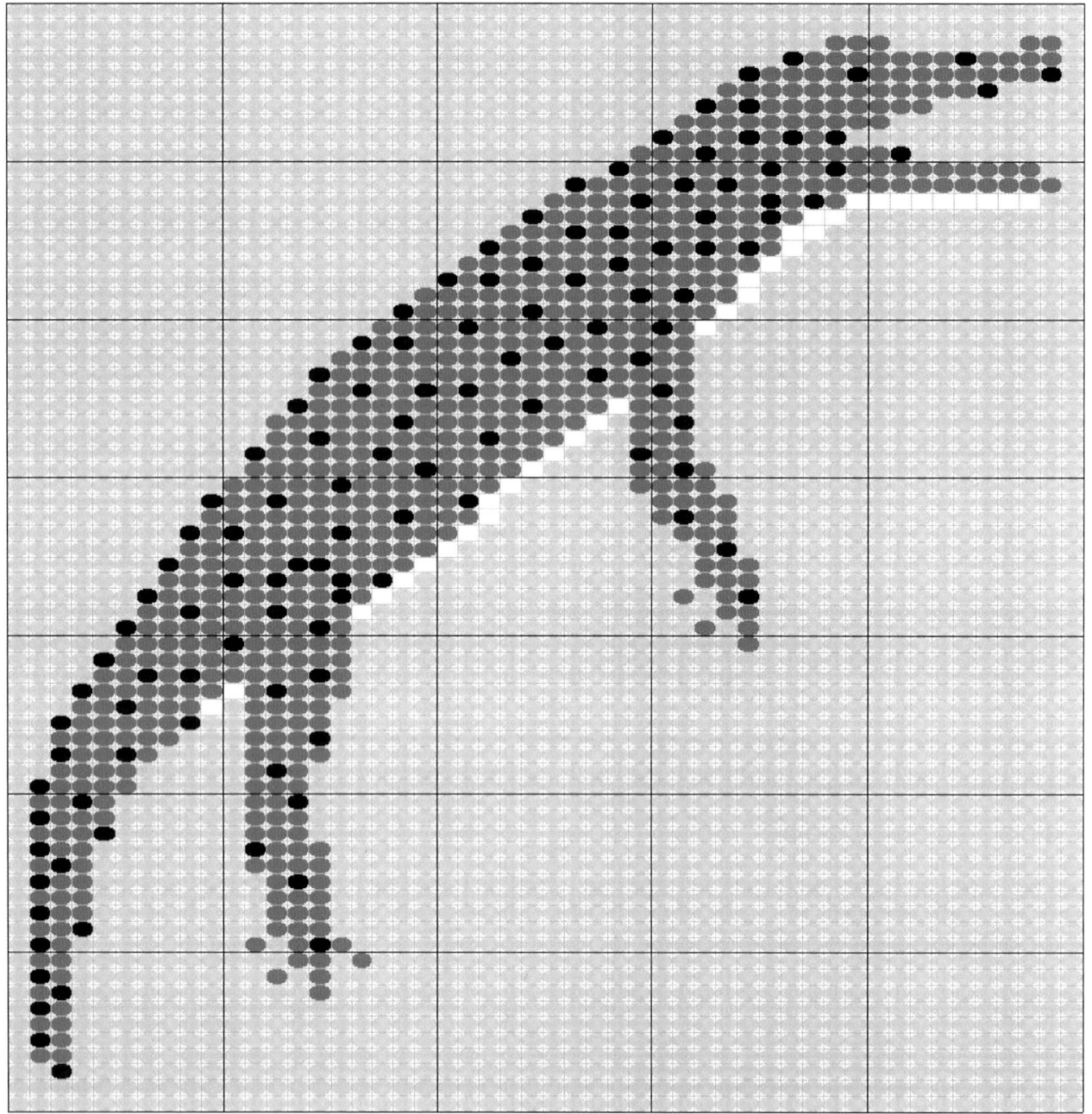

YARN COLORS

Light blue, white, black and gray.

SAND DOLLAR
GRAPH / CHART

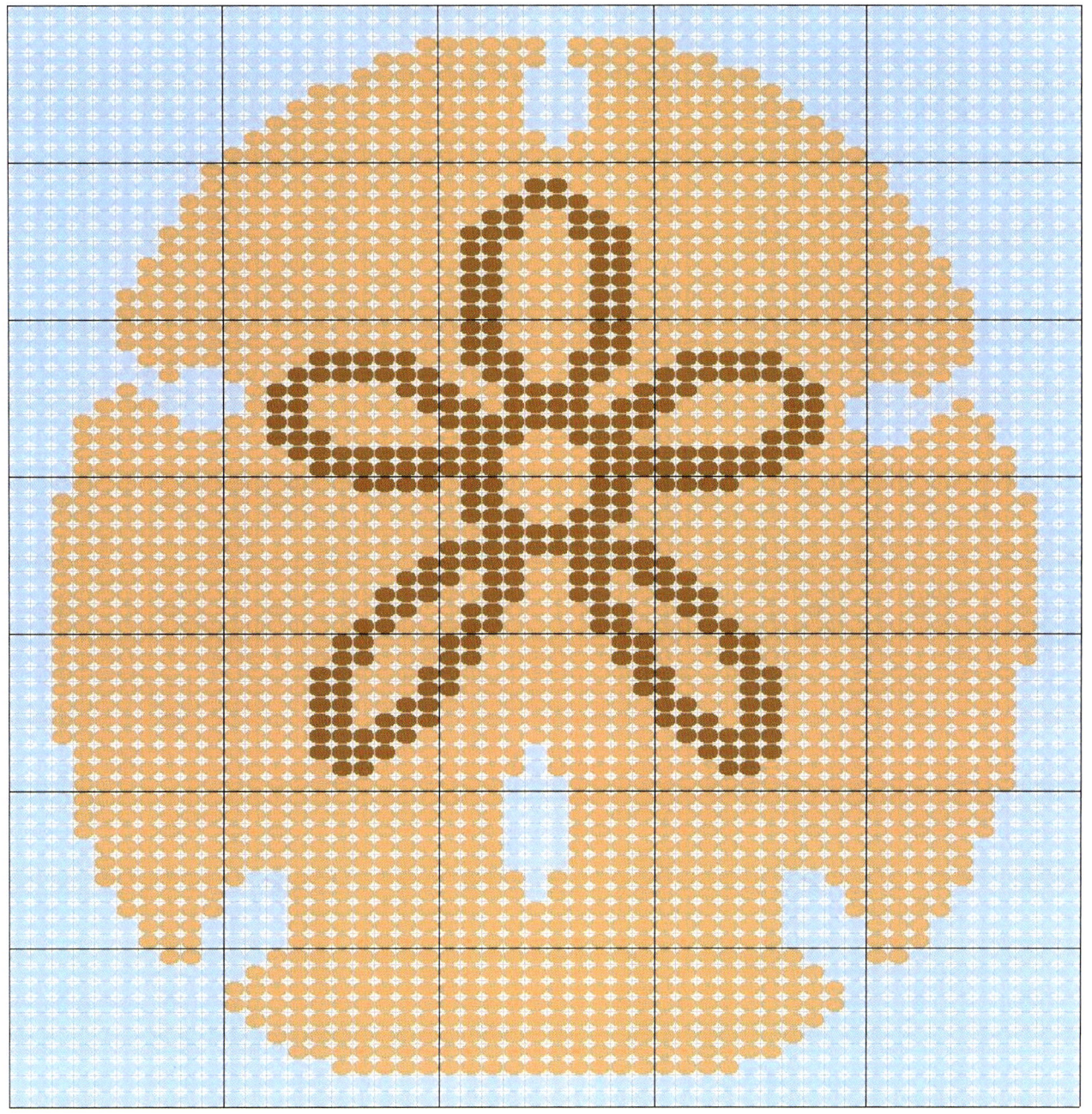

YARN COLORS

Light blue, brown, and tan.

SEA ANEMONE
GRAPH / CHART

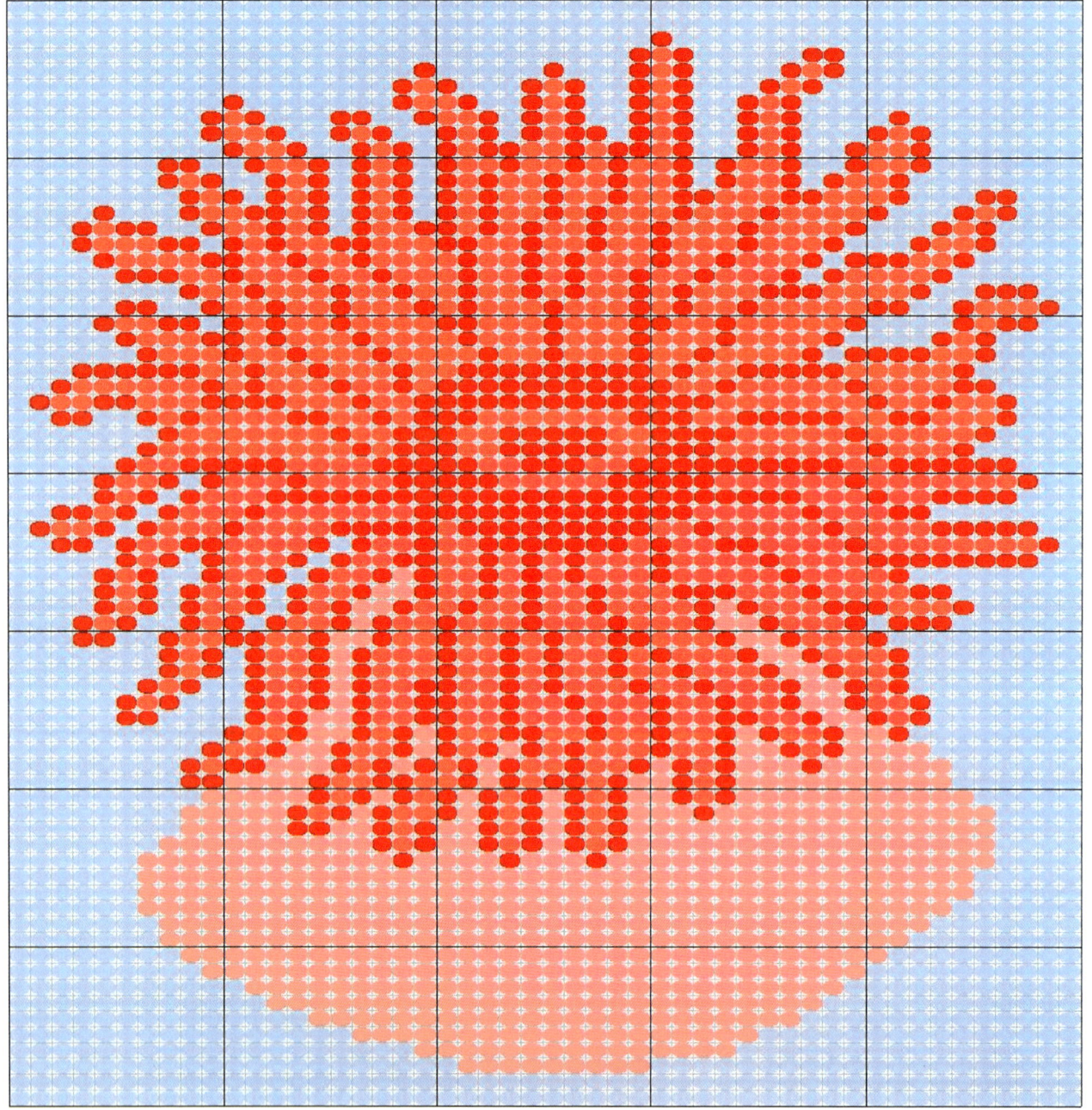

YARN COLORS

Light blue, pink, dark pink/salmon and red.

SEA CUCUMBER
GRAPH / CHART

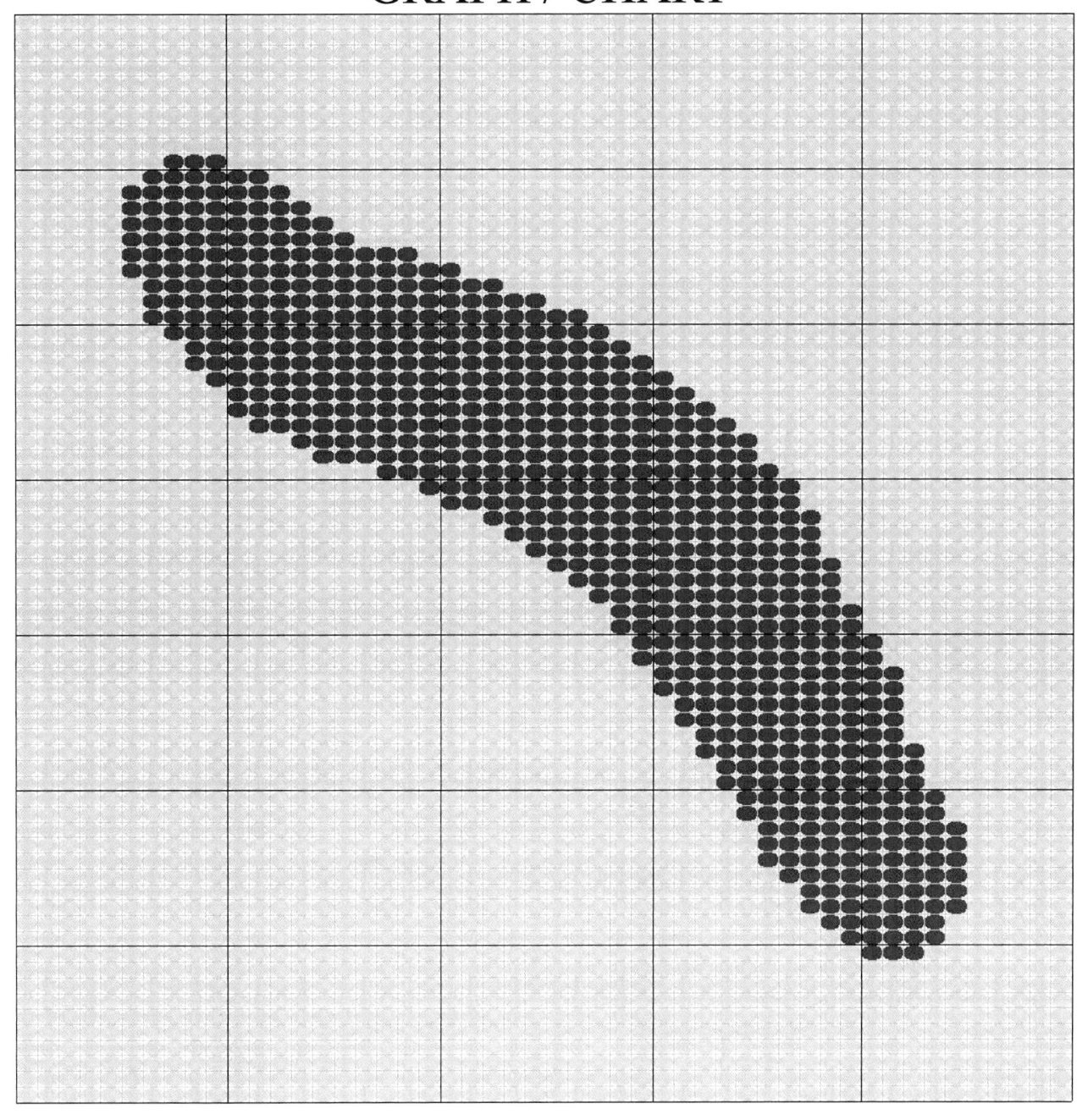

YARN COLORS

Light blue and forest green.

SEA HORSE
GRAPH / CHART

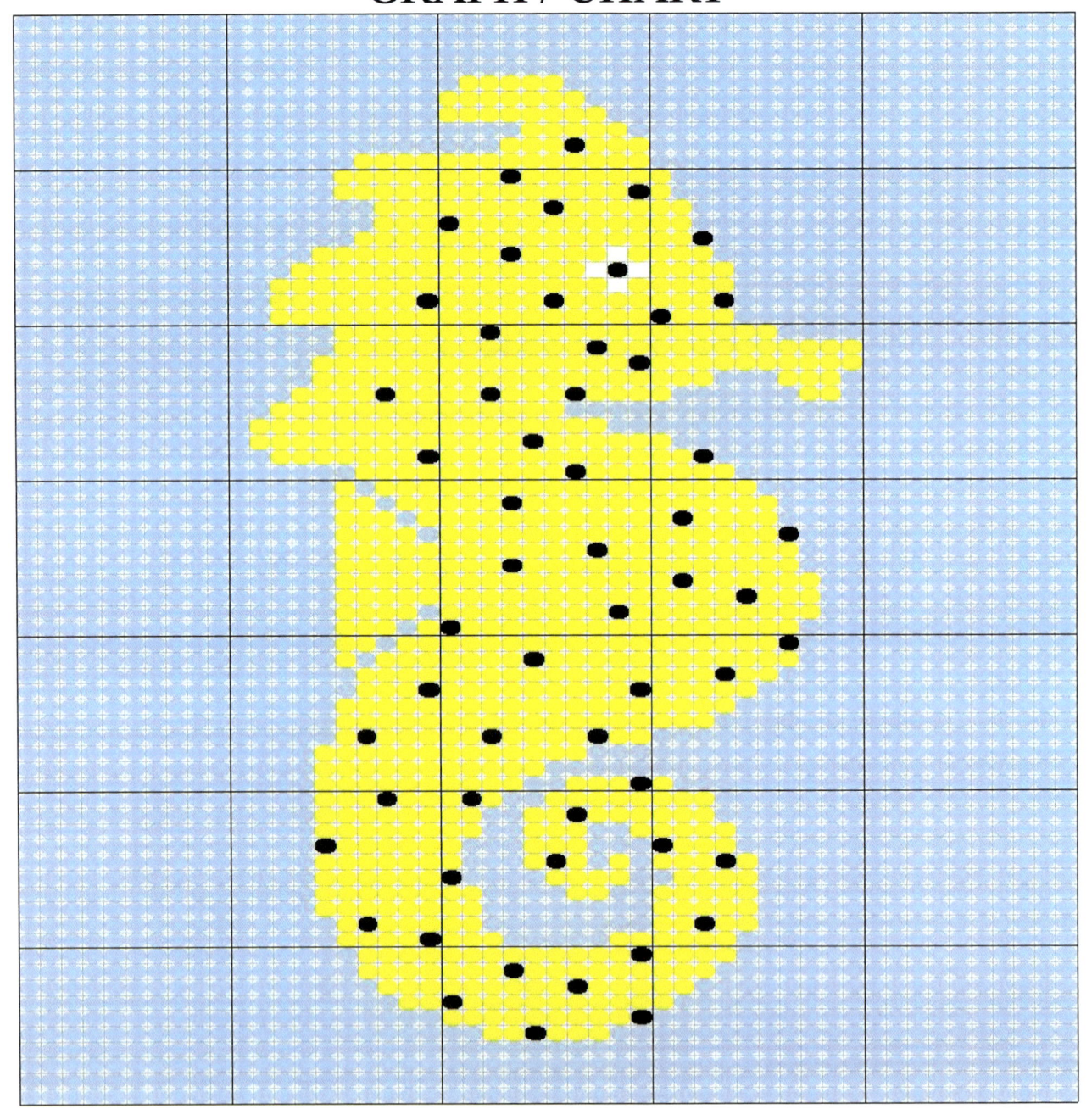

YARN COLORS

Light blue, yellow, white and black.

SEA SNAIL
GRAPH / CHART

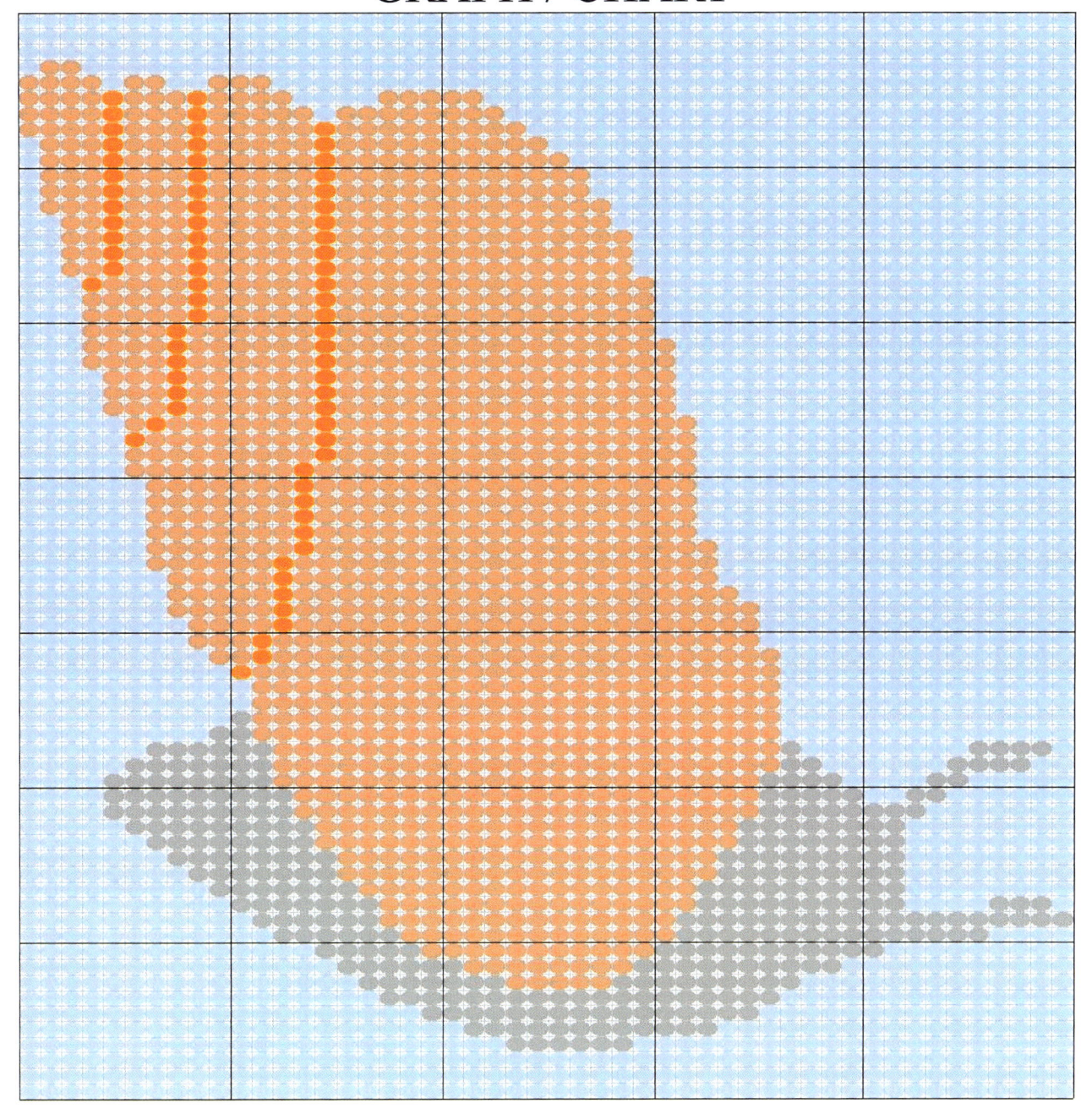

YARN COLORS

Light blue, gray, tan and orange.

SEA SNAKE
GRAPH / CHART

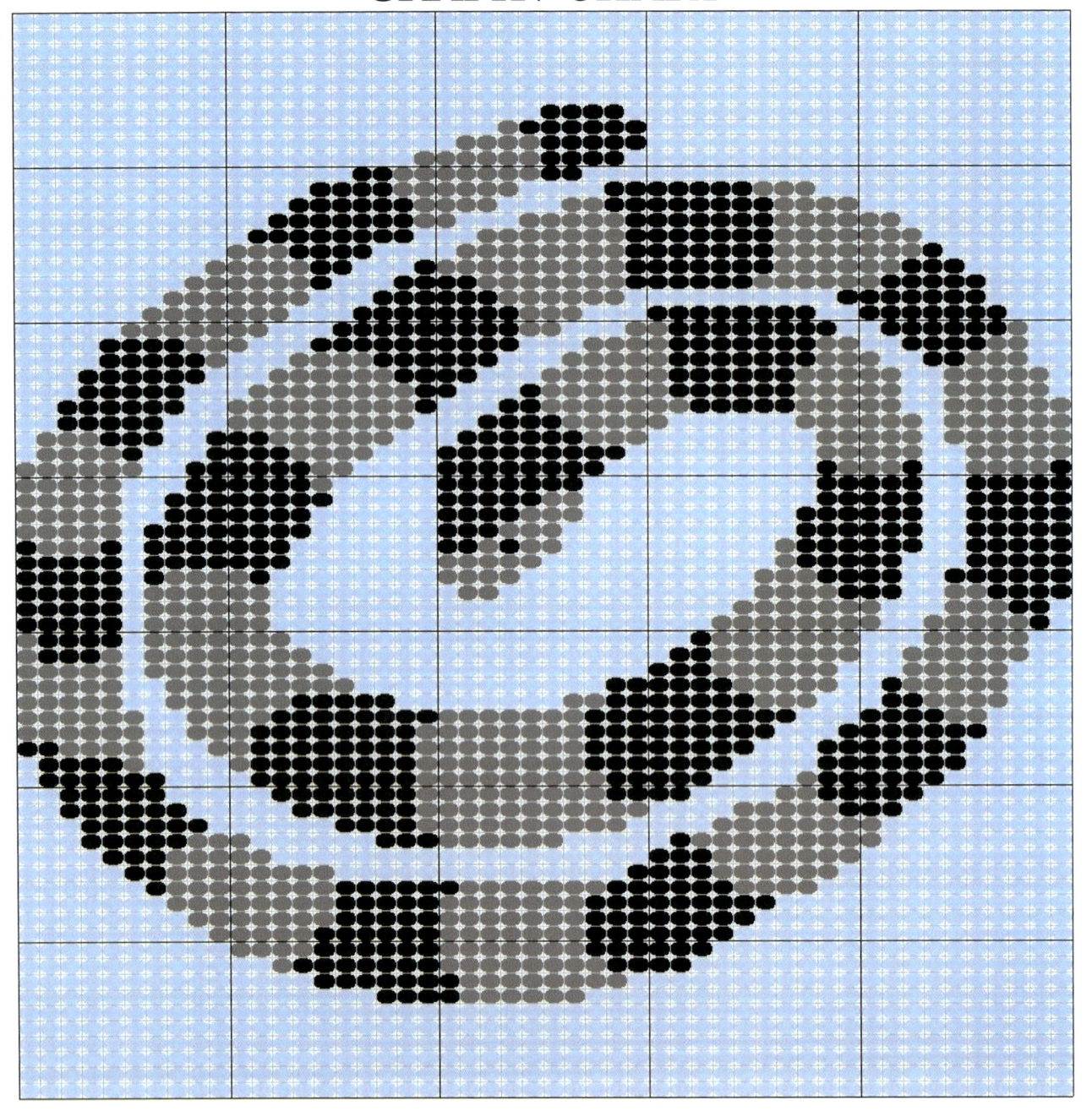

YARN COLORS

Light blue, black, and gray.

SEA TURTLE
GRAPH / CHART

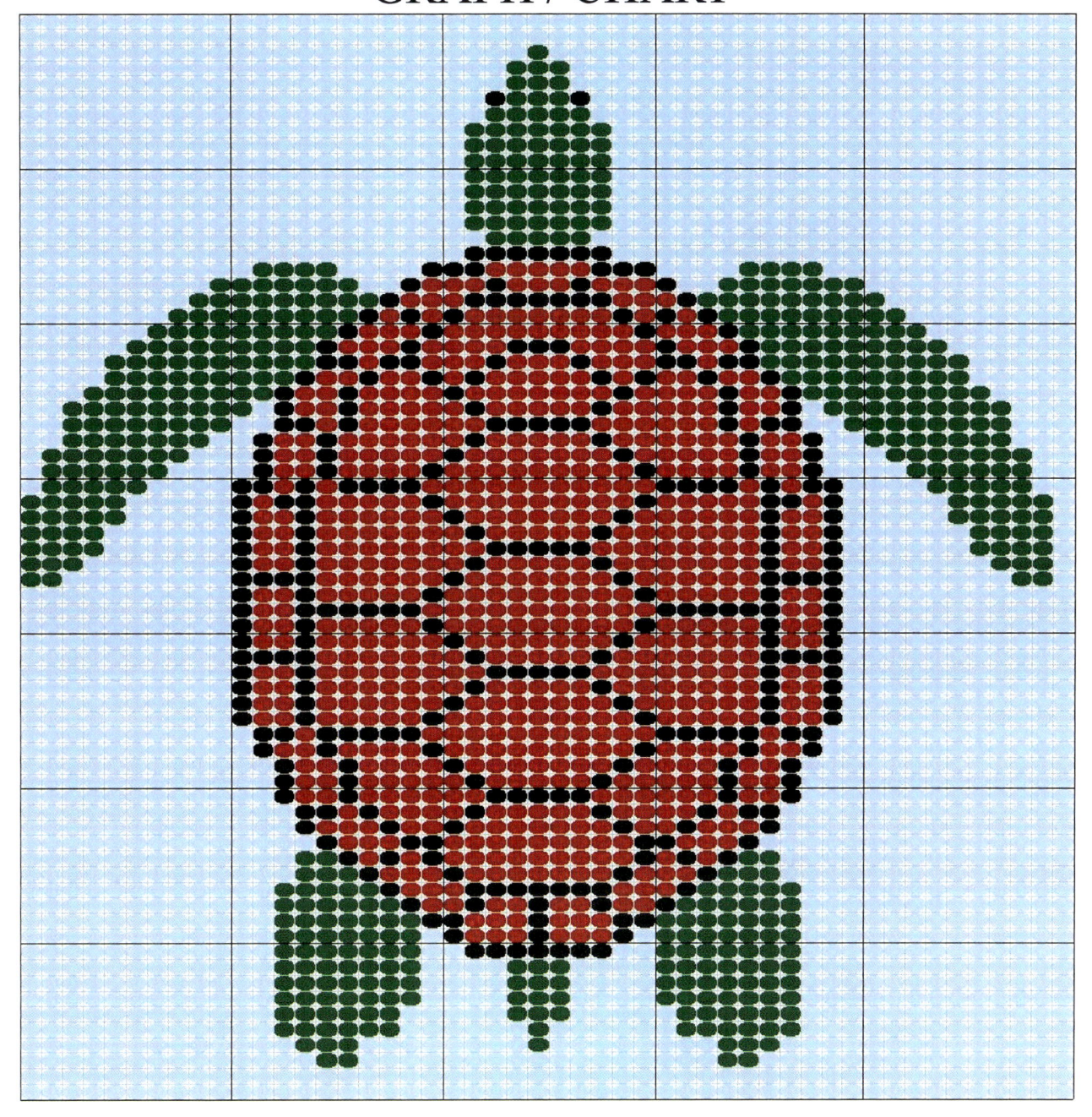

YARN COLORS

Light blue, green, black and dark red/rust.

SEA URCHIN
GRAPH / CHART

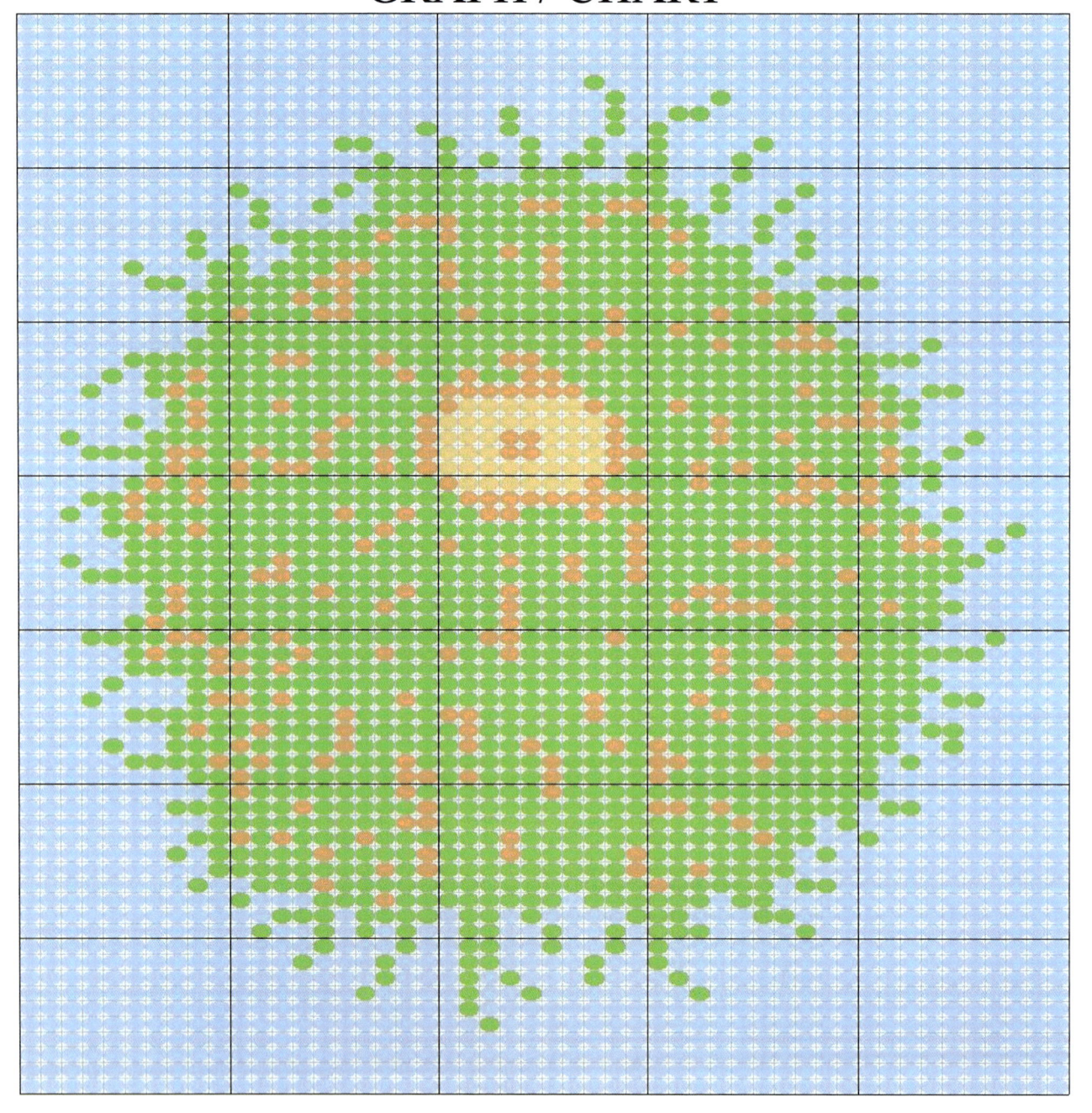

YARN COLORS

Light blue, medium green, tan and light tan.

SEA WORM
GRAPH / CHART

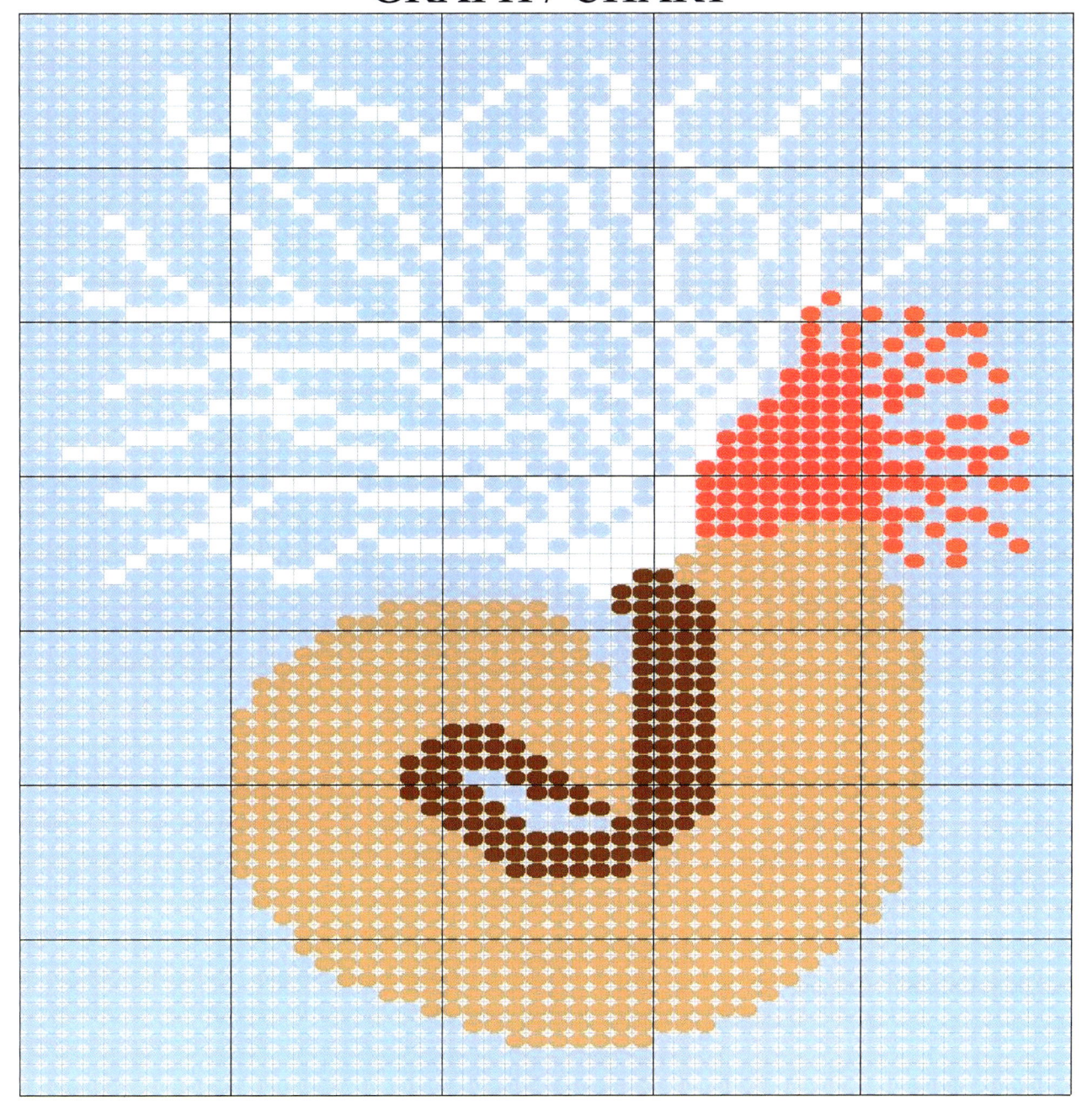

YARN COLORS

Light blue, white, pink, light brown and dark brown.

SHARK (Great White)
GRAPH / CHART

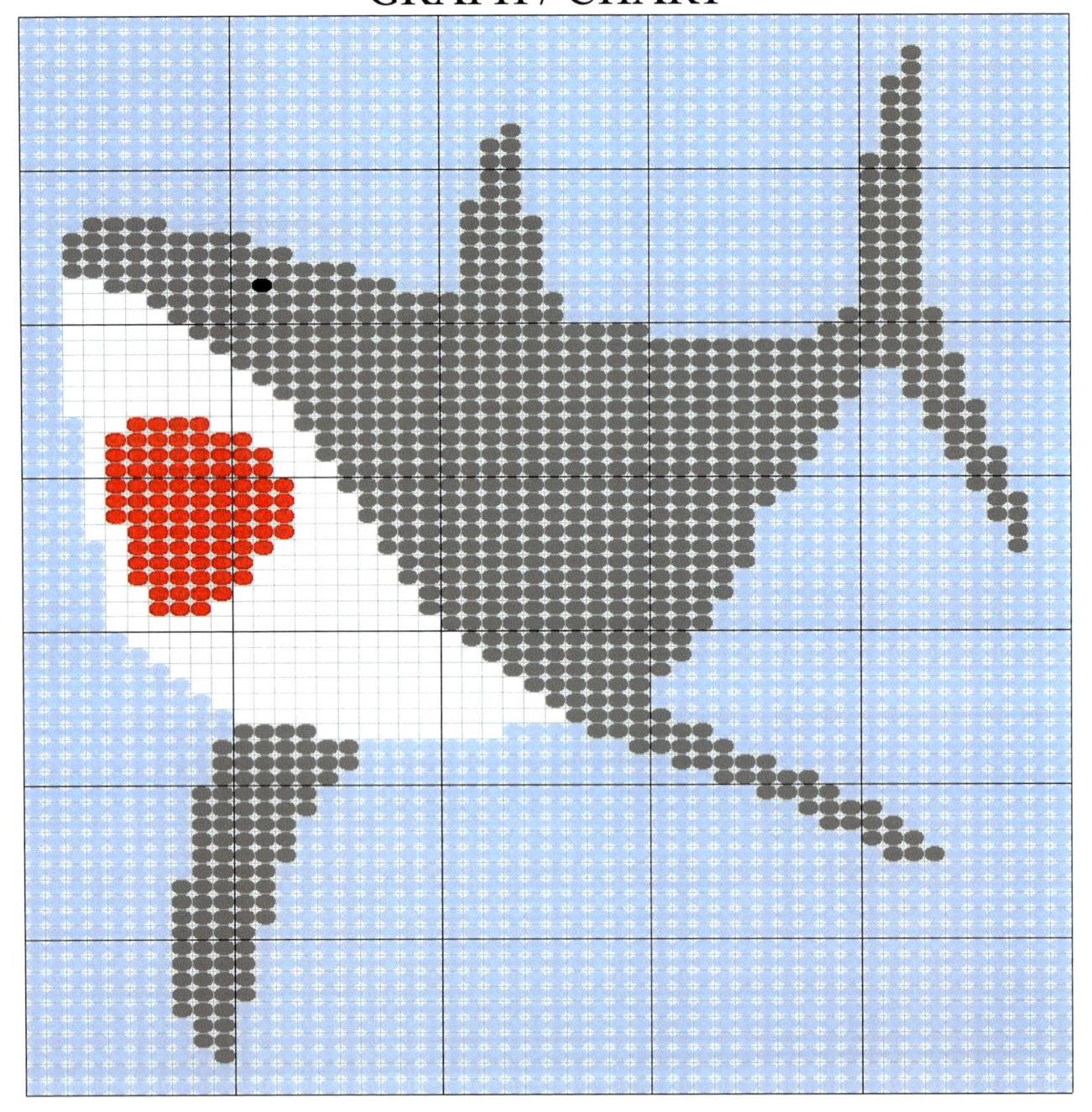

YARN COLORS

Light blue, black, white, gray and red.

SHRIMP
GRAPH / CHART

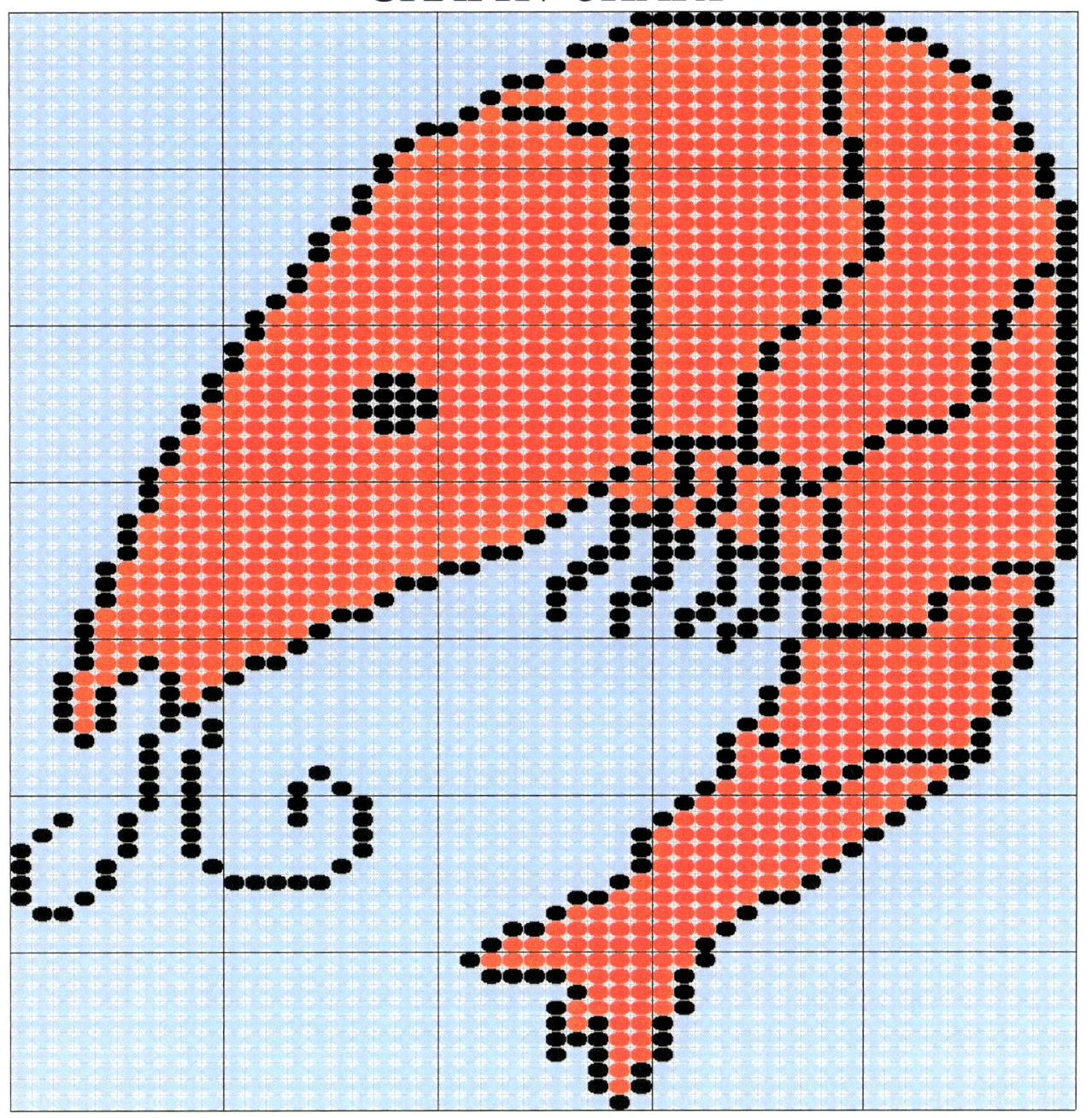

YARN COLORS

Light blue, black, and dark pink/salmon.

SQUID
GRAPH / CHART

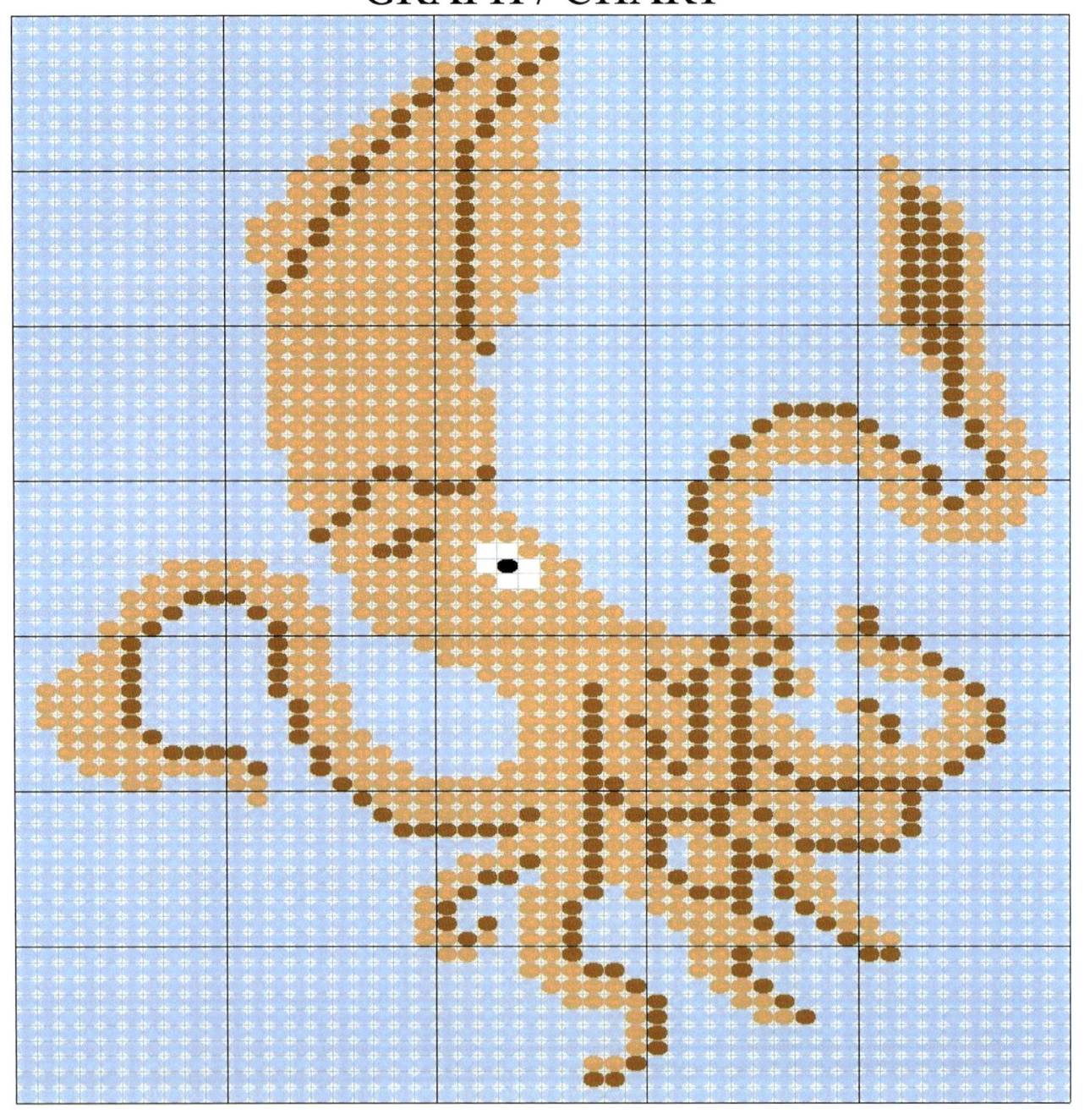

YARN COLORS

Light blue, light brown, brown, white and black.

STARFISH
GRAPH / CHART

YARN COLORS

Light blue, light orange and orange.

STINGRAY
GRAPH / CHART

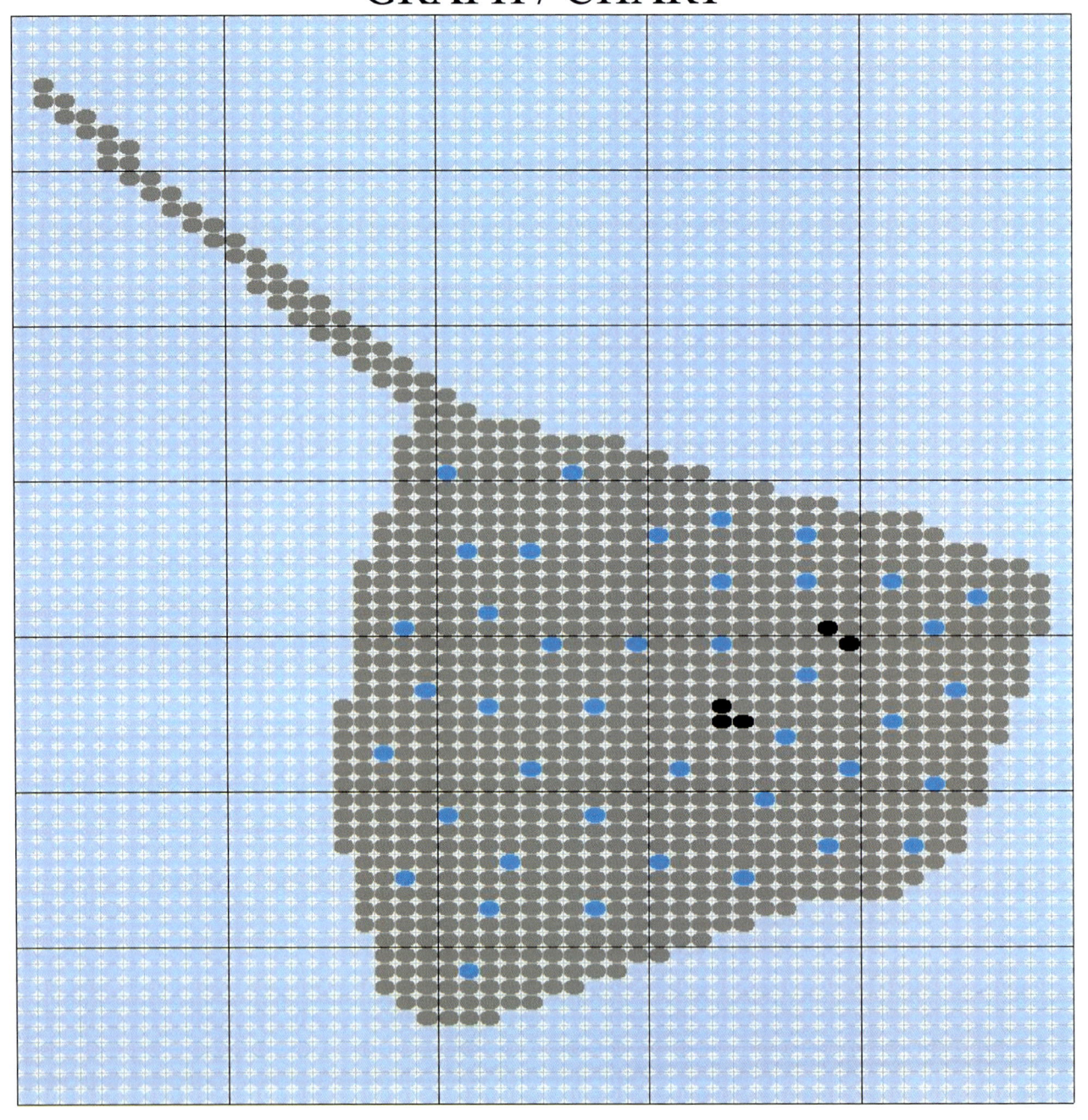

YARN COLORS

Light blue, blue, gray and black.

NOTES: